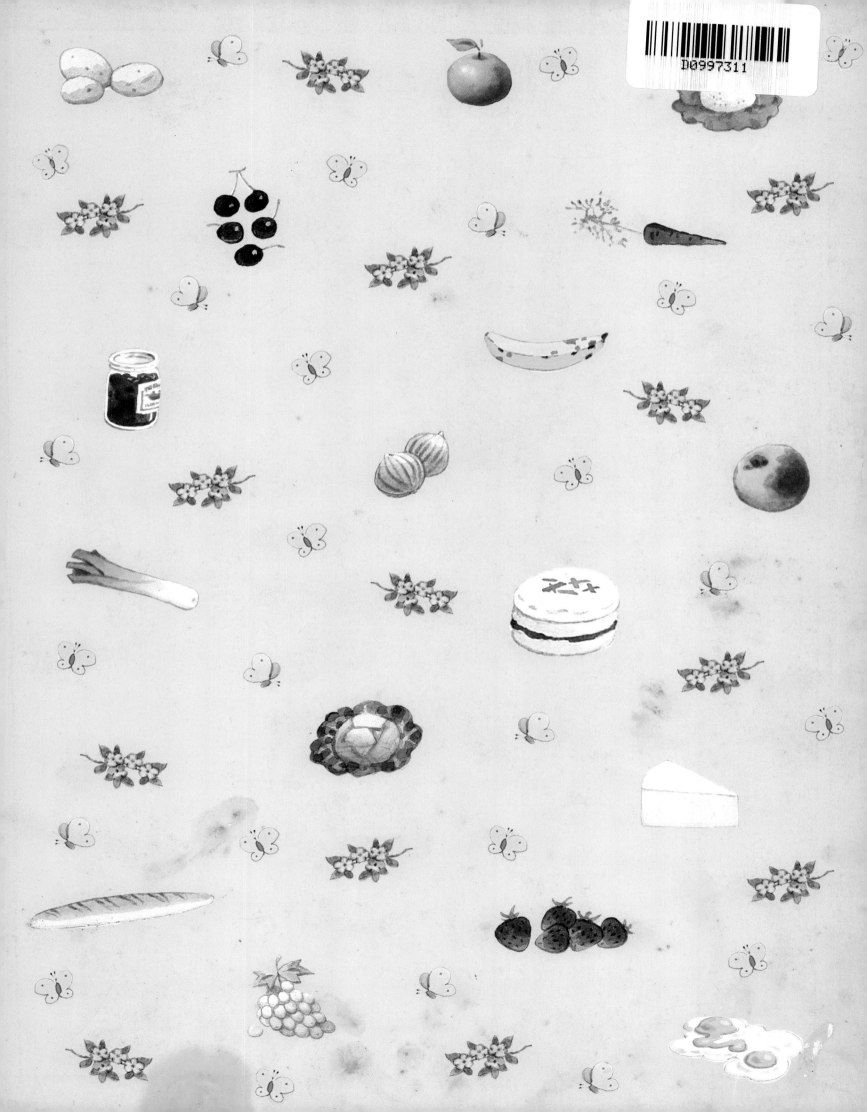

The Usborne

Farmyard Tales
Children's Cookbook

Fiona Watt

Illustrated by Stephen Cartwright
and Molly Sage

TED SMART

Recipes by Catherine Atkinson, Roz Denny

and Julia Kirby Jones

Designed by Helen Wood
Photography by Howard Allman

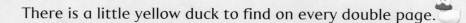

There is a little yellow duck to find on every double page.

This is Apple Tree Farm.

Mr. Boot and Mrs. Boot live here with their two children, Poppy and Sam. They have a dog called Rusty and a cat called Whiskers. Ted drives the tractor and helps look after all the animals on the farm.

Contents

Below each list of ingredients, you can find out how long each recipe will keep for. Some of them need to be eaten on the day they are made, but others will keep for a few days. If you're not sure of some of the cooking words, turn to pages 46-47 where you will find tips and explanations which will help you.

Cheese and tomato tarts

Makes six tarts

375g (13oz) packet of ready-rolled
   puff pastry
1 tablespoon of milk
1 large onion
3 tablespoons of olive oil
half a teaspoon of dried mixed herbs
salt and ground black pepper
225g (8oz) cherry tomatoes
225g (8oz) mozzarella cheese

Heat your oven to 220°C, 425°F, gas mark 7.

Eat the tarts after they have
cooled for a few minutes.

Trim the
pastry to fit
the baking sheet.

1. Turn on your oven.
Unroll the pastry and put
it on a baking sheet. Trim
one end off if you need to,
then cut it into six pieces.

2. Put the milk into a cup.
Use a pastry brush to
brush the milk around the
edges of the pieces, to
make a 1cm (½in) border.

3. Cut the ends off the
onion and peel off the
skin. Cut the onion in
half, then carefully cut
each half into thin slices.

If you like olives, scatter
one or two on each tart
with the tomatoes.

You can also add courgettes to these tarts.

Slice a medium courgette and add it to the pan, halfway through cooking the onion at step 4.

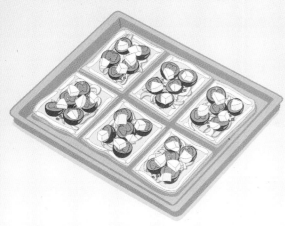

4. Heat the olive oil over a low heat and add the pieces of onion. Cook gently for ten minutes until the onion is soft.

5. Stir in the mixed herbs and add some salt and pepper. Spoon the onion over the pastry, but do not cover the milky border.

6. Use a serrated knife to cut the tomatoes in half. Arrange the tomatoes on top of the mixture, with their cut sides upwards.

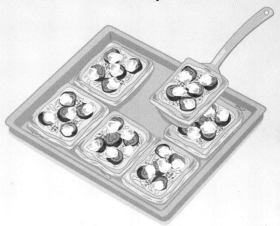

7. Open the bag of cheese and pour away any liquid. Cut the cheese into 1cm (½in) cubes. Scatter them evenly over the tomatoes.

8. Put the baking sheet on the middle shelf of the oven for 25-30 minutes, until the pastry rises and turns brown.

9. Leave the tarts on the baking sheet for about three minutes to cool a little. Then, serve the tarts immediately.

Marshmallow crispies

Makes about 12 pieces

100g (4oz) toffee
100g (4oz) butter or margarine
100g (4oz) marshmallows
100g (4oz) rice crispies

a 28 x 18cm (11 x 7in) shallow tin

🦋 Storage: Keep in an
airtight container and eat
within four days.

They will take
about 15
minutes
to melt.

1. Grease the tin with butter
on a paper towel. If you
have a slab of toffee, put it
in a plastic bag and break
it up with a rolling pin.

2. Put the toffee and butter
or margarine into a pan.
Add the marshmallows.
Melt them gently over a low
heat, stirring all the time.

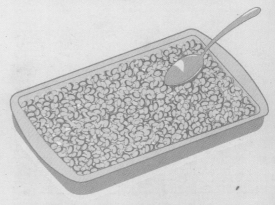

3. When everything has
melted and blended
together, take the pan
off the heat. Gently stir
in the rice crispies.

4. Spoon the mixture into
the tin and press it gently
with the back of a metal
spoon. Leave the mixture
to set, then cut it up.

Corn flake crunch

Makes eight pieces

225g (8oz) milk or plain chocolate
3 tablespoons of golden syrup
50g (2oz) margarine
100g (4oz) corn flakes

a 20cm (8in) shallow round tin

Storage: Keep in an airtight container and eat within four days.

1. Grease the tin with a little butter or margarine on a paper towel. Grease the inside well, but do not leave on too much butter.

2. Break the chocolate into a large pan. Add the syrup and margarine. Heat the pan gently, stirring the mixture all the time.

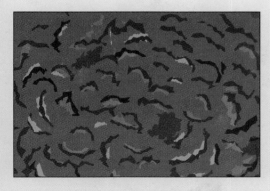

Lift the pieces out with a blunt knife or a pie slice.

3. When the chocolate has melted, add the corn flakes and stir them well. Make sure that they are coated all over with chocolate.

4. Spoon the mixture into the tin. Carefully smooth the top with the back of a spoon. Try not to crush the corn flakes.

5. Put the tin in a fridge for the chocolate to set. It will take about two hours. Then, use a sharp knife to cut it into eight pieces.

Poppy's tasty pancakes

Makes about 12 pancakes

100g (4oz) plain flour
a pinch of salt
1 egg
sunflower oil
300ml (½ pint) milk

You can leave the pancake mixture until you are ready to use it, but stir it before making your pancakes. Eat them straight away.

Use a whisk to beat it.

1. Put a sieve over a large mixing bowl. Pour in the flour and the salt. Shake the sieve until all the flour has fallen through.

2. Press a whisk into the middle of the flour to make a deep hollow. Break an egg into a cup, then pour it into the hollow.

3. Add a tablespoon of oil and two tablespoons of milk. Beat the egg, oil and milk with some of the flour from around the hollow.

Eat the pancakes with maple syrup, or lemon juice and caster sugar. You can also spread them with honey, chocolate spread or jam.

4. Add some more milk and beat it again. Continue to add some milk and beat it, until all the milk is mixed in and the batter is smooth.

5. Heat a small frying pan over a medium heat for about a minute. Don't put anything into the pan at this point.

6. Put two tablespoons of oil into a cup. Roll up a paper towel and dip one end into it. Wipe oil quickly over the bottom of the pan.

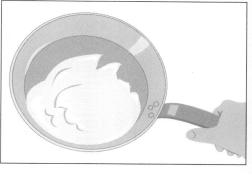

7. Quickly add three tablespoons of batter. Swirl it all over the bottom by tipping the pan. The batter should sizzle.

8. Put the pan on the heat and cook the ba until it turns pale and is lightly cooked. Small holes will also appear on the top.

9. Loosen the edge of the pancake and slide a spatula under it. Flip the pancake over and cook it for half a minute more.

Make a stack of pancakes under the tea towel.

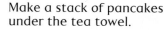
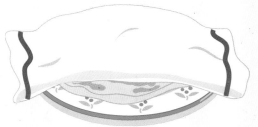

10. Slide the pancake onto a plate, then cover it with a clean tea towel. Make more pancakes, following steps 6 to 9.

Farmyard biscuits

Makes about 18 biscuits

350g (12oz) plain flour
2 teaspoons of ground ginger
1 teaspoon of bicarbonate of
  soda
100g (4oz) butter
175g (6oz) soft light brown sugar
1 egg
4 tablespoons of golden syrup

large farm animal cookie
  cutters

Heat your oven to 180°C, 350°F,
gas mark 4.

 Storage: Keep in an airtight
container and eat within five days.

1. Dip a paper towel in some margarine and rub it over two baking sheets to grease them. Then, turn on your oven.

2. Sift the flour, ginger and bicarbonate of soda into a mixing bowl. Cut the butter into chunks and add it to the bowl.

3. Rub the butter into the flour with your fingertips, until the mixture looks like fine breadcrumbs. Then, stir in the sugar.

4. Break the egg into a small bowl. Add the syrup to the egg, then use a fork to beat them together well.

5. Stir the eggy mixture into the flour. Mix everything together with a metal spoon until it makes a soft dough.

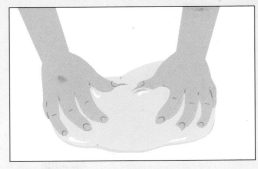

6. Sprinkle a clean work surface with flour and put the dough onto it. Stretch the dough by pushing it away from you.

7. Fold the dough in half. Turn it and push it away from you again. Continue to push, turn and fold until the dough is smooth.

8. Cut the dough in half. Sprinkle a little more flour onto your work surface. Roll out the dough until it is about 5mm (¼in) thick.

9. Use cookie cutters to cut out lots of shapes from the dough. Then, lift the shapes onto the baking sheets with a fish slice.

10. Roll out the other half of dough and cut shapes from it. Squeeze the scraps to make a ball. Roll it out and cut more shapes.

Spread the shapes out on the baking sheets.

11. Put the the baking sheets into your oven and bake them for 12-15 minutes. They will turn golden brown.

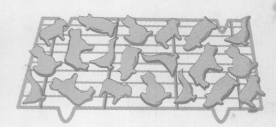

12. Leave the biscuits on the sheets for about five minutes. Then, lift them onto a wire rack. Leave them to cool.

Sam and Poppy's muffins

Makes 12 muffins

250g (9oz) self-raising flour
pinch of salt
1 teaspoon of baking powder
50g (2oz) butter
75g (3oz) soft light brown sugar
100g (4oz) chocolate chips
2 eggs
2 teaspoons of vanilla essence or extract
250ml (8floz) milk

a 12-hole deep bun or muffin tin

Heat your oven to 200°C, 400°F, gas mark 6.

Eat straight away, or keep in an airtight container and eat within three days.

1. Dip a paper towel into some butter or margarine and rub it inside the holes in the tin. Then, put a paper muffin case in each hole.

2. Turn on your oven. Put a sieve over a large bowl. Then, shake the flour, salt and baking powder through the sieve.

3. Cut the butter into small pieces and add it to the flour mixture. Rub the butter into the flour until it looks like breadcrumbs.

4. Add the light brown sugar and about three-quarters of the chocolate chips. Stir them in until they are mixed in evenly.

5. Break the eggs into a medium-sized bowl and beat them with a fork. Add the vanilla essence and milk, then beat it again.

6. Pour the egg mixture into the flour in one go. Mix it quickly with a fork to blend everything. It should still look a little lumpy.

7. Spoon some mixture into each paper case, filling it almost to the top. Sprinkle the remaining chocolate chips on top.

8. Bake the muffins in the oven for about 20 minutes until the muffins have risen in the paper cases and the tops are firm.

9. Leave the muffins in the tin for about five minutes, then lift them onto a wire rack. Serve them while they are still warm.

For double chocolate muffins, use 225g (8oz) of self-raising flour and 25g (1oz) of cocoa powder.

Sam's favourite soup

Serves four to six

250g (9oz) potatoes
2 medium leeks
25g (1oz) butter
1 tablespoon of oil
1 stock cube
dried mixed herbs
300ml (½ pint) milk
salt and ground black pepper

🦋 Eat straight away.

1. Use a vegetable peeler to peel the potatoes. Then, cut the peeled pieces into small chunks. Put them into a large pan.

2. Cut the roots and the dark green tops off the leeks. Slice through the outside layer of each leek, then peel it off.

3. Wash the leeks thoroughly under cold running water. Make sure that there is no dirt left between the layers.

4. Slice the leeks into 1cm (½in) pieces. Put the leeks, butter and oil into the pan with the potatoes and stir everything well.

5. Turn on the heat and slowly melt the butter. When it starts to sizzle, put a lid on the pan and turn the heat down low.

6. Let the vegetables cook gently for ten minutes. Shake the pan occasionally to stop it from sticking, but don't lift the lid.

Stir until the stock cube dissolves.

7. Meanwhile, boil some water. Put the stock cube into a measuring jug. Pour in 900ml (1½ pints) of boiling water and stir it.

8. When the vegetables are cooked, carefully pour in the stock. Add a pinch of mixed herbs, the milk and a little salt and pepper.

9. Turn up the heat and bring the soup to the boil. Then, turn the heat down so that the soup is bubbling gently.

10. Let the soup cook for about 15 minutes more. Then, use a ladle to serve the soup straight away into bowls.

Sprinkle each bowl of soup with some chopped parsley and serve it with warm bread rolls (see pages 44-45).

Delicious lemon cake

Makes about 12 slices

1 lemon
225g (8oz) self-raising flour
1 teaspoon of baking powder
4 eggs
225g (8oz) soft margarine
225g (8oz) caster sugar

For the filling:
75g (3oz) caster sugar
2 eggs
1 lemon
50g (2oz) unsalted butter

For the icing:
1 lemon
125g (5oz) icing sugar

two 20cm (8in) round tins

Heat your oven to 180°C, 350°F,
  gas mark 4.

✿✿ Storage: this is best eaten
on the day it is made, but you
can store it for up to two days
in airtight container in a fridge.

1. Draw around the tins on baking parchment or greaseproof paper. Cut out the circles and put them in the tins. Grease the tins.

2. Turn on your oven. Grate the rind off a lemon, then cut it in half. Twist each half on a lemon squeezer to squeeze out the juice.

3. Sift the flour and baking powder into a bowl. Break the eggs into a cup, then add them, along with the margarine and sugar.

4. Beat everything in the bowl well, then stir in the lemon rind and lemon juice. Divide the mixture between the two tins.

5. Bake the cakes for 25 minutes, until they spring up when you press them in the middle. Then, leave them on a rack to cool.

6. While the cakes are cooling, make the filling. Put the caster sugar into a heatproof bowl. Break the eggs and add them.

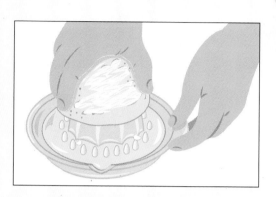

7. Grate the rind off a lemon and squeeze the juice from it. Add the rind and juice to the bowl. Cut the butter into pieces and add it, too.

8. Put some water into a pan and turn on the heat so that the water is just bubbling. Lower the bowl into the pan.

9. Stir the mixture with a wooden spoon as it thickens. Take it off the heat when it coats the back of a metal spoon and leave it to cool.

10. Spread one of the cakes with the filling. Put the other cake carefully on top. Don't worry if some of the filling oozes out.

A zester gives you long pieces of rind.

Press hard as you scrape.

11. Grate some rind off the remaining lemon, or scrape some off with a zester. Keep the rind on one side for decorating the cake.

Stir in the juice a little at a time.

12. To make the icing, squeeze half of the lemon. Sift the icing sugar. Pour in the juice until it is like glue. Ice and decorate the cake.

Poppy's 'pizzas'

Serves two

1 onion
2 cloves of garlic
2 tablespoons of olive oil
400g (14oz) can of chopped tomatoes
half a teaspoon of dried mixed herbs
salt and ground black pepper
1 ciabatta bread
250g (9oz) mozzarella cheese
2 tablespoons of grated Parmesan cheese
a selection of toppings such as ham, olives,
    pepperoni, salami, cherry tomatoes

Heat your oven to 200°C, 400°F, gas mark 6.

Eat straight away.

1. Cut the top and bottom off the onion and peel the skin off it. Cut it in half and slice it. Peel the garlic cloves and crush them.

2. Heat the oil in a frying pan. Gently cook the garlic and onion, for five minutes, or until they are soft, stirring once or twice.

3. Add the tomatoes, the dried herbs and some salt and pepper. Turn up the heat and bring the mixture to the boil.

4. Turn the heat down to medium and let the mixture cook for about ten minutes, or until most of the liquid has gone.

5. Take the frying pan off the heat. Leave the mixture to cool for 10-15 minutes. Meanwhile, turn on your oven to heat up.

6. Put the bread onto a chopping board and cut it in half lengthways. Put the two halves onto a large baking sheet.

7. Spread each piece of bread with the topping. Slice the mozzarella cheese as finely as you can and lay the slices on top.

8. Add any other toppings you want, then sprinkle Parmesan cheese on top. Bake the 'pizzas' for about 15 minutes.

9. Take the baking sheet out of the oven and let the 'pizzas' cool for five minutes. Cut each half into pieces, to make it easier to eat.

Try one with cheese, pepperoni and olives.

Apple crumble

Serves six

500g (1lb) eating apples
6 tablespoons of water
ground cinnamon
1 tablespoon of caster sugar

For the topping: 100g (4oz) plain flour
100g (4oz) wholemeal flour
100g (4oz) butter
75g (3oz) light soft brown sugar

Heat your oven to 180°C, 350°F, gas mark 4.

✿ This is best served hot and
eaten straight away.

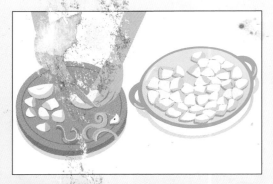

1. Cut the apples into
quarters. Peel them, then
cut out the cores. Cut the
pieces into chunks. Put
them in a pie dish.

2. Add the water. Sprinkle
the apples with a large
pinch of cinnamon and
a tablespoon of caster
sugar. Turn on your oven.

3. Stir both types of flour
together in a mixing bowl.
Then, cut the butter into
small pieces and put it in
the bowl with the flour.

4. Mix the flour and butter
with a blunt knife. Stir and
cut the flour again and
again until each piece of
butter is coated with flour.

5. Wash your hands and
dry them really well.
Rub the butter into the
flour. Lift the mixture
and let it fall as you rub.

6. When the mixture
looks like coarse
breadcrumbs, mix in the
soft brown sugar. Mix it
in with your fingers, too.

You could use plums or blackberries instead of apples to make this crumble.

7. Sprinkle the topping over the apple. Spread it out evenly with a fork and smooth the top. Put the dish onto a baking sheet.

8. Bake the crumble for 45 minutes, until the top is golden. Turn the crumble around halfway through, so that it browns evenly.

9. To check that it is cooked, push a knife into a piece of apple. If it's not soft, cook the crumble for five more minutes.

10. Leave the crumble to cool for at least five minutes before you serve it. Serve it with cream or ice cream.

Mrs. Boot's special cherry cake

Makes about eight slices

150g (5oz) glacé cherries
200g (7oz) self-raising flour
175g (6oz) soft margarine
175g (6oz) caster sugar
50g (2oz) ground almonds*
3 eggs

a loaf tin measuring
  20 x 12 x 8cm (8 x 5 x3½in)

Heat your oven to 180°C, 350°F,
  gas mark 4.

Storage : the cake will keep
for four days if you wrap it in
greaseproof paper, then in foil or
put it in an airtight container.

Instead of cherries you could use
other dried fruit, such as dried
apricots.

* Don't give this cake to anyone
who is allergic to nuts

Use kitchen scissors
to cut the cherries.

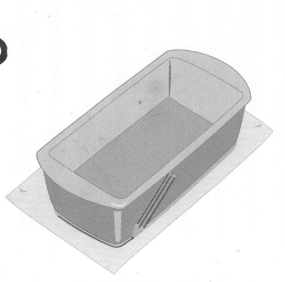

1. Cut each cherry into
quarters. Put them in a
sieve and rinse them under
warm running water. Pat
them dry on a paper towel.

2. Put the loaf tin onto
baking parchment or
greaseproof paper. Draw
around the bottom of the
tin and cut out the shape.

3. Grease the bottom and
sides of the tin with some
margarine on a paper
towel. Put the paper into
the tin. Turn on your oven.

4. Sift the flour into a bowl. Add the margarine, sugar and ground almonds. Break the eggs into a cup, then pour them in too.

5. Beat the mixture firmly with a wooden spoon, until it is light and fluffy. Gently fold in the pieces of cherry with a metal spoon.

6. Scrape the mixture out of the bowl into the loaf tin. Smooth the top with the back of a spoon to make it level.

When you slice the cake, the cherries are scattered through each piece.

7. Bake the loaf for about 1¼ hours, until it rises and turns golden. Leave it for a few minutes, then turn it onto a wire rack.

8. When the cake is completely cold, put it onto a cutting board. Use a bread knife to cut it into about eight slices.

Ted's salads

Each salad serves four

For the lemon and honey dressing:
5 tablespoons of sunflower oil
1½ tablespoons of lemon juice
1 teaspoon of clear honey
salt and ground black pepper

For the potato salad:
750g (1lb 10oz) small new potatoes
2 sticks of celery
2 small red-skinned dessert apples
6 stems of fresh chives

For the garden salad:
2 little, or baby, gem lettuces
half a cucumber
225g (8oz) baby plum or cherry
tomatoes
2 medium carrots

 Eat straight away.

Lemon and honey dressing

Put the lid on the jar before you shake it.

For the dressing, put the oil, lemon juice, honey and a pinch of salt and pepper into a jar which has a screw top. Shake it well.

Potato salad

Wait until the potatoes are cool enough to handle.

1. For the potato salad, scrub the potatoes. Boil them for about 15 minutes, until they are cooked. Drain them and cut them in half.

Leave the rest of the dressing in the jar.

2. Put the potatoes in a large bowl, and pour half of the dressing over them while they are still warm. Leave them to cool.

Garden salad

3. Wash the celery and slice it into thin slices. Cut the apples into quarters and cut out the cores. Cut the apples into small chunks.

4. Using kitchen scissors, snip the chives into small pieces. Add the celery, apples and chives to the bowl. Mix everything well.

1. For the garden salad, pull the leaves off the lettuces. Rinse them well, shake them dry, then tear them into pieces.

2. Put the lettuce leaves in a large bowl. Slice the cucumber finely. Use a serrated knife to cut the tomatoes in half.

Serve the salads in a big bowl or as individual portions on plates.

3. Peel the carrots and cut them in half. Then, cut them into very thin strips. Add the tomatoes, carrots and cucumber to the bowl.

4. Shake the rest of the dressing in the jar, and pour it over the garden salad. Then, gently mix everything together.

Sam's shortbread

Makes eight pieces

150g (5oz) plain flour
25g (1oz) ground rice or rice flour
100g (4oz) butter, refrigerated
50g (2oz) caster sugar

a 20cm (8in) shallow round tin

Heat your oven to 170°C, 325°F,
   gas mark 3.

Storage: keep in an airtight
container and eat within five days.

1. Turn on your oven to
heat it up. Dip a paper
towel into some butter,
then rub it over the
inside of the tin.

2. Put a sieve over a large
mixing bowl and pour the
flour and ground rice, or
rice flour, into it. Shake
them into the bowl.

3. Cut the butter into small
pieces and put them into
the bowl. Mix the pieces
with a blunt knife to coat
them with flour.

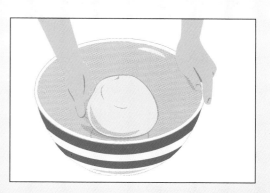

4. Rub the pieces of butter between your fingertips. Lift the mixture and let it fall back into the bowl as you rub.

5. Carry on rubbing in the butter until the mixture looks like breadcrumbs. Stir in the caster sugar with a wooden spoon.

6. Holding the bowl in one hand, squeeze the mixture into a ball. The heat from your hand will make the mixture stick together.

Cut across it again, before lifting it out.

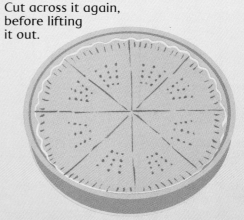

7. Press the mixture into the tin with your fingers, then use the back of a spoon to press down the top and make it level.

8. Use the prongs of a fork to press a pattern around the edge. Then, cut the mixture into eight equal pieces with a blunt knife.

9. Bake it for 30 minutes, until it becomes golden. Leave the shortbread for five minutes before putting it on a wire rack.

Mrs. Boot's best carrot cake

Makes 8 to 12 slices

250g (9oz) carrots
150g (5oz) butter
2 large eggs
200g (7oz) light soft brown sugar
200g (7oz) self-raising flour
half a teaspoon of salt
2 teaspoons of ground cinnamon
2 teaspoons of baking powder
75g (3oz) chopped walnuts*
2 tablespoons of milk

For the topping:
50g (2oz) icing sugar
200g (7oz) cream cheese
1 tablespoon of lemon juice
half a teaspoon of vanilla
    essence or extract

a 28 x 18 cm (11 x 7in) shallow
    cake tin

Heat your oven to 180°C, 350°F,
    gas mark 4.

🦋 Storage: keep in a sealed
container in a refrigerator and
eat within three days.

* Don't give these to anyone
who is allergic to nuts.

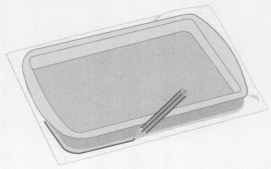

1. Put your cake tin onto a piece of greaseproof paper or baking parchment and draw around it. Cut out the shape you have drawn.

2. Brush the sides and the base of tin with a little vegetable oil to grease it. Put the paper inside and brush it with oil, too.

3. Turn on your oven. Wash the carrots and cut off their tops. Grate them on the side of the grater with the biggest holes.

4. Put the butter into a pan and heat it gently until it has just melted. Pour the melted butter into a large bowl.

5. Break the eggs into a small bowl and beat them. Stir the carrots and sugar into the melted butter. Then, add the beaten eggs.

6. Put a sieve over the bowl. Shake the flour, salt, cinnamon and baking powder through the sieve, onto the mixture.

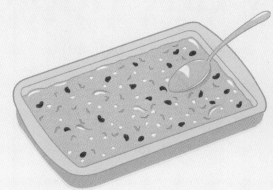

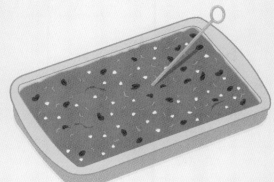

7. Use a wooden spoon to beat the mixture, until it is smooth. Add the walnuts, then stir in two tablespoons of milk.

8. Spoon the mixture into the tin. Smooth the top with a spoon. Tap the tin on your work surface to make the mixture level.

9. Bake the cake for 45 minutes. Test it by sticking a skewer into it. When it comes out it should have no mixture sticking to it.

Peel the paper off the bottom of the cake.

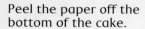

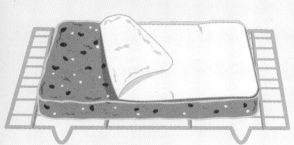

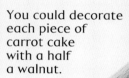

You could decorate each piece of carrot cake with a half a walnut.

10. Leave the cake for ten minutes to cool. Then, run a knife around the sides of the cake and turn the cake out onto a wire rack.

11. While the cake is cooling, sift the icing sugar into a bowl. Add the cheese, lemon juice and vanilla. Beat the mixture well.

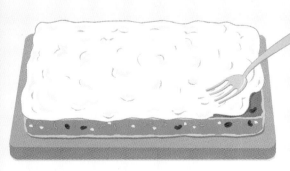

12. When the cake has cooled, spoon the topping onto it. Spread the topping with a fork, making lots of swirly patterns.

Rainy day flapjacks

Makes 12 flapjacks

175g (6oz) margarine
175g (6oz) demerara sugar
2 tablespoons of golden syrup
225g (8oz) porridge oats

a 18 x 27cm (7 x 11in) shallow tin

Heat your oven to 160°C, 325°F,
gas mark 3.

Storage: Keep in an airtight container and eat within a week.

The syrup will slide off a hot spoon more easily than a cold one.

1. Turn on your oven. Put the tin onto baking parchment or greaseproof paper and draw around the bottom of the tin.

2. Cut out the rectangle of paper and put it into the tin. Then, grease it with some margarine on a paper towel.

3. Put the margarine into a large pan and add the sugar. Dip a tablespoon into hot water then use it to add the syrup.

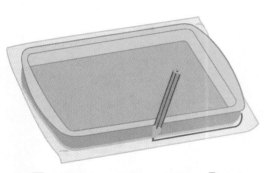

4. Heat the mixture gently, until the margarine has melted. Stir it with a wooden spoon, but don't allow the mixture to boil.

5. Take the pan off the heat. Then, add the oats. Stir them in really well so that they are covered in the syrup mixture.

6. Spoon the flapjack mixture into the tin and spread it all over the bottom. Push the mixture well into the corners.

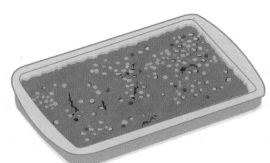

Cut the flapjacks while they are in the tin and still warm.

7. Smooth the mixture with the back of a spoon. Then, put on oven gloves and put the tin on the middle shelf of your oven.

8. Bake the mixture for about 25 minutes. The flapjacks are ready when the oats have turned golden brown.

9. Take the tin out of the oven and leave it for ten minutes. Cut the mixture into pieces. Leave them in the tin until they are cold.

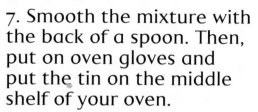
It's best to cut the flapjacks into squares while they are still warm and in the tin.

Strawberry trifle

Serves four

500g (1lb) fresh strawberries
6 trifle sponges
2 tablespoons of strawberry jam
4 tablespoons of apple juice
1 small lemon
300ml (½ pint) double cream
2 tablespoons of milk
half a teaspoon of vanilla essence or extract
2 tablespoons of caster sugar

Storage: The trifle is best eaten on the day you make it, but any leftovers can be covered with plastic foodwrap and stored in a fridge for up to two days.

Leave a few strawberries for the top of your trifle.

1. Pull the stalks out of the strawberries. Try to pull out them out with the core still attached. Use a small knife if you need to.

2. Cut most of the strawberries in half, or in quarters if they are very big. Put the pieces into a medium-sized bowl.

3. Cut the sponges in half. Spread each half with jam then press them back together again. Cut the sponges into quarters.

4. Put the pieces of sponge on top of the strawberries and mix them gently. Trickle the apple juice over them.

5. Cover the bowl with plastic foodwrap and put it into a fridge for about three hours. The sponges will go soft.

6. Grate the yellow rind, or zest, from the lemon, using the medium holes on a grater. Then, use a knife to scrape off the zest.

7. When the sponge mixture is nearly chilled, put the cream into a large bowl. Add the milk, lemon zest, vanilla and sugar.

Instead of making the trifle in one bowl, you can make individual servings in smaller bowls.

8. Beat the mixture with a whisk until it becomes slightly stiff. Don't beat it too hard as it will become too solid to spread.

9. Spread the creamy mixture over the sponges and strawberries. Put the trifle in a fridge until you are ready to serve it.

Macaroni cheese

Serves four

175g (6oz) dried macaroni

For the cheese sauce:
50g (2oz) butter
50g (2oz) plain flour
600ml (1 pint) milk
175g (6oz) Cheddar or Gruyère cheese, grated
salt and pepper

For the topping:
25g (1oz) Cheddar or Gruyère cheese, grated

Heat your oven to 180°C, 350°F, gas mark 4.

Eat straight away.

Serve the macaroni cheese with
lettuce and cucumber, or the
garden salad from pages 24-25.

Pour the macaroni back into the pan after it has drained.

Add a pinch of salt and pepper too.

1. Turn on your oven. Put the macaroni into a pan. Cook it following the instructions on its packet. Drain it when it's cooked.

2. To make the sauce, melt the butter in a pan over a low heat. Stir in the flour with a wooden spoon and cook it for one minute.

3. Take the pan off the heat and add a little milk. Stir it really well. Carry on stirring in the rest of the milk, a little at a time.

4. Return the pan to the heat and start to bring it to the boil, stirring all the time. The sauce will stick if you don't stir it.

5. The sauce will begin to thicken. Let the sauce bubble for a minute then turn off the heat. Stir in the cheese.

6. Pour the sauce over the cooked macaroni. Stir it really well so that the sauce coats all of the pieces of macaroni.

7. Dip a paper towel into some margarine and rub it inside an ovenproof dish to grease it. Pour in the cheesy macaroni.

8. Sprinkle on grated cheese for the topping. Put the dish into the oven for about 25 minutes, until the top is golden brown.

Chocolate brownies

Makes 15 brownies

175g (6oz) margarine
350g (12oz) caster sugar
1 teaspoon of vanilla essence or extract
3 eggs
125g (5oz) plain flour
1 level teaspoon of baking powder
50g (2oz) cocoa
175g (6oz) walnuts*

a 22 x 30 x 2.5cm (9 x 12 x 1in) oblong tin

Heat your oven to 180°C, 350°F, gas mark 4.

Storage: Keep in an airtight container and eat within a week.

* Don't give these to anyone who is allergic to nuts.

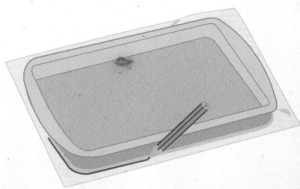

1. Put your tin onto a piece of greaseproof paper or baking parchment. Draw around it and cut out the rectangle.

2. Grease the tin with some margarine on a paper towel. Lay the paper in the tin and grease the top of it. Then, turn on your oven.

3. Put the margarine into a pan and melt it over a low heat. Pour it into a mixing bowl, then add the sugar and vanilla.

Beat the mixture each time you add some egg.

4. Break the eggs into a small bowl and beat them. Add them to the large bowl, a little at a time. Beat them in well.

5. Sift the flour into the bowl and add the baking powder and the cocoa. Stir everything together so that it is mixed well.

6. Put the walnuts onto a chopping board and cut them into small pieces. Add them to the mixture and stir it well again.

7. Pour the mixture into the tin and smooth the top with the back of a spoon. Bake it for about 40 minutes.

8. The brownies are ready when they have risen and a crust has formed on top. They should still be soft in the middle.

Use a fish slice to lift them.

9. Leave the brownies in the tin for five minutes, then cut them into 15 squares. Leave them on a wire rack to cool.

Poppy's favourite chocolate cake

Makes about 12 slices

2 teaspoons of sunflower oil
250g (9oz) self-raising flour
6 tablespoons of cocoa powder
2 teaspoons of baking powder
300g (10oz) sunflower margarine
   (not low-fat spread)
300g (10oz) soft brown sugar
2 teaspoons of vanilla essence or
   extract
6 large eggs
150g (5oz) dark chocolate
150ml (¼ pint) double cream

two 20cm (8in) round cake tins

Heat your oven to 170°C, 325°F,
   gas mark 3.

✿ Storage: This is best eaten
on the day you make it.

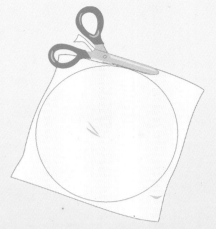

1. Turn on your oven. Put the cake tins onto baking parchment or greaseproof paper and draw around them. Cut out the circles.

Use a pastry brush.

2. Brush sunflower oil over the inside of the tins. Put a paper circle in the bottom of each one, then brush the paper with oil.

3. Hold a sieve over a large bowl and sift the flour, cocoa and baking powder through it. Get out another mixing bowl.

Use a wooden spoon.

4. Put the margarine and sugar into the empty bowl and beat until they are creamy. Add the vanilla and beat it again.

Don't forget to add a tablespoon of flour with each egg.

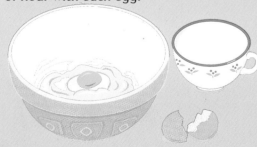

5. Crack one egg into a cup and add it to the bowl with one tablespoon of flour. Beat well. Repeat this with each egg.

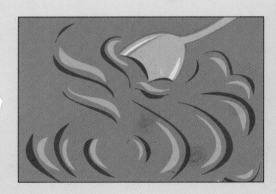

6. Gently stir in the rest of the flour, moving the spoon in the shape of a number eight. This will keep the mixture light.

Use a knife to make the top level.

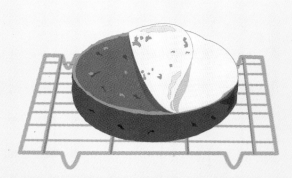

7. Put the mixture into the cake tins. Put them on the middle shelf of the oven. Cook for 40-45 minutes. Test them with a skewer.

8. When the cakes are cooked, leave them to cool for five minutes. Then, run a knife around the side of each tin.

9. Turn each tin upside down over a wire rack and shake it. The cakes should pop out. Peel off the paper and leave them to cool.

10. For the icing, break the chocolate into a heatproof bowl. Add the cream. Heat 5cm (2in) of water in a pan until it is just bubbling.

11. Put the bowl in the pan. Stir the chocolate as it melts. When it has melted, let it cool, then put the bowl into the fridge.

12. Stir the icing a few times while it is cooling in the fridge. It will thicken. When it is like soft butter, take it out of the fridge.

The cake is very rich, so don't cut it into huge slices.

13. Spread a third of the icing on one cake. Put the other cake on top of it and cover the top and sides with the icing.

Picnic cookies

Makes about 12 cookies

100g (4oz) caster sugar
100g (4oz) butter
1 egg
half a teaspoon of vanilla essence or extract
175g (6oz) plain flour
175g (6oz) milk or plain chocolate chips

Heat your oven to 180°C, 350°F, gas mark 4.

❀ Storage: Keep in an airtight container and eat within five days.

1. Grease two baking sheets by dipping a paper towel into butter or margarine. Rub it over the baking sheets. Turn on your oven

2. Put the caster sugar and the butter into a large mixing bowl. Stir them together really well with a wooden spoon.

3. Carry on stirring them together briskly. You are trying to get the mixture as smooth and creamy as you can.

4. Break the egg into a small bowl and beat it well. Pour the vanilla into a measuring spoon, then mix it in with the egg.

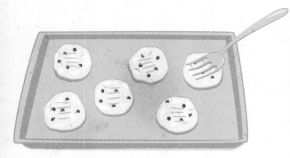

Use a wooden spoon.

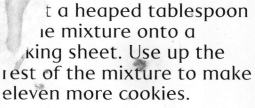

5. Pour the eggy mixture into the mixing bowl and stir it in. Then, sift the flour into the bowl and stir the mixture.

6. When you have a smooth mixture, stir in 100g (4oz) of the chocolate chips. You'll use the rest of them later.

7. Put a heaped tablespoon of the mixture onto a baking sheet. Use up the rest of the mixture to make eleven more cookies.

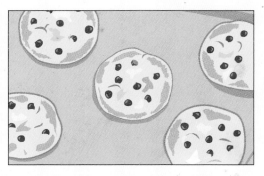

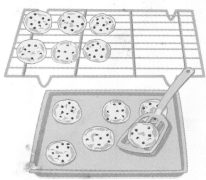

8. Flatten each cookie slightly with the back of a fork. Sprinkle the top of each one with some of the remaining chocolate chips.

9. Bake the cookies for 10-15 minutes, until they are pale golden brown. They should still be slightly soft in the middle.

10. Leave the cookies for a few minutes, then use a spatula or fish slice to lift them onto a wire rack. Leave them to cool.

Orange biscuits

Makes about 60 biscuits

150g (5oz) butter
200g (7oz) plain flour
quarter of a teaspoon of salt
2 teaspoons of baking powder
1 large egg
200g (7oz) caster sugar
1 teaspoon of vanilla essence or extract
2 oranges

Heat your oven to 200°C, 400°F, gas mark 6.

Storage: Keep in an airtight container for up to five days. This makes a lot of biscuits, but you don't need to use it all in one go (see step 9).

1. Weigh the butter and leave it for about an hour to soften. Sift the flour, salt and baking powder into a bowl.

2. Break the egg into a cup or small bowl. Beat it briskly with a fork, so that the yolk and the white are mixed well.

3. Put the butter and sugar into another bowl and beat them until they are creamy. Stir in the egg and the vanilla.

Scrape the zest off the grater with a knife.

4. Grate the skin, or zest, off the oranges using the medium holes on a grater. Stir the zest into the creamy mixture.

5. Add the flour and stir it until you get a smooth dough. If the dough feels very soft, put it into a fridge for an hour.

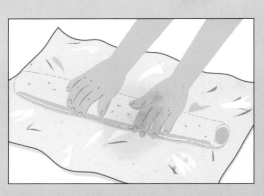

6. Put a long piece of foil onto your work surface and scrape the dough onto it. Roll the dough to make a long sausage shape.

7. Wrap the foil around the dough and put it in a fridge for about an hour, until it becomes firm. Turn on your oven.

8. Take the dough out of the fridge and cut it into very thin slices. You don't need to use all the dough at one time.

9. If you don't want to use all the dough, wrap it in foil. It will keep for about ten days in a fridge or up to six weeks in a freezer.

10. Spread out the slices of dough on a non-stick baking sheet. Bake them for about seven minutes, until they are golden.

11. Leave the biscuits on the baking sheet for one minute, then use a fish slice to slide them onto a wire rack to cool.

Bread rolls

Makes 16 rolls

450g (1lb) strong white bread flour
1½ teaspoons of salt
2 teaspoons of caster sugar
1½ teaspoons of easy-blend dried yeast
275ml (9floz) milk
25g (1oz) butter
1 egg

Heat your oven to 220°C, 425°F, gas mark 7.

These are best eaten on the day you make them.

You can sprinkle poppy seeds or sesame seeds onto the rolls after brushing them with egg (see step 11).

1. Shake the flour and salt through a sieve into a large bowl. Stir in the sugar and yeast, then make a hollow in the middle.

Stir it with a wooden spoon.

The mixture should be lukewarm, not hot.

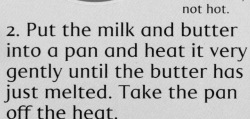

2. Put the milk and butter into a pan and heat it very gently until the butter has just melted. Take the pan off the heat.

3. Pour the milk mixture into the hollow in the flour. Stir it until it is all mixed and no longer sticks to the side of the bowl.

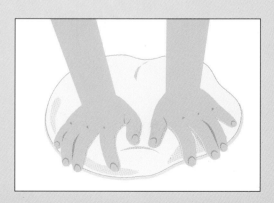

4. Sprinkle some flour onto a clean, dry work surface. Knead the dough by pushing it away from you with both hands.

5. Fold the dough in half and turn it around. Then push it away from you again. Fold and turn it, then push it away again.

6. Knead the dough until it is smooth and stretchy. Dip a paper towel in oil, then rub it inside a bowl. Put the dough in the bowl.

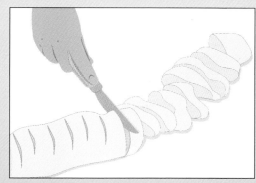

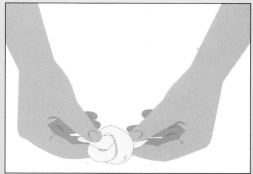

7. Cover the bowl with plastic foodwrap. Leave it in a warm place for about 45 minutes, until the dough has risen to twice its size.

8. Knead the dough again for about a minute, to burst any large bubbles of air in it. Then, divide the dough into 16 pieces.

9. Roll each piece of dough to make a 'sausage' about 25cm (10in) long. Tie each one into a knot and put it on a greased baking sheet.

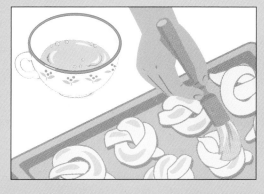

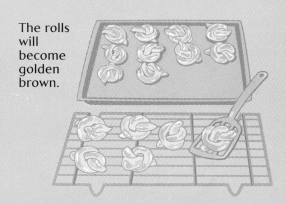

The rolls will become golden brown.

10. Turn on your oven. Rub some plastic foodwrap with oil, then cover the rolls. Put them back in a warm place for 20 minutes.

11. Beat the egg in a small bowl, then take the foodwrap off the rolls. Brush each roll with some of the beaten egg.

12. Bake the rolls for 10-12 minutes. Leave them on the baking sheets for a few minutes, then leave them to cool on a wire rack.

Cooking tips

If you haven't done much cooking before, some of the cooking techniques in this book may be new to you, so you may need some help. These two pages explain some of the cooking words which are used in the book.

Measuring spoons

Use measuring spoons to measure ingredients in tablespoons or teaspoons. They give you exactly the amount you need.

Sifting

You need to sift some ingredients, such as flour, to get rid of lumps. Put the flour in a sieve over a bowl and gently shake the sieve.

Adding eggs

When a recipe asks you to add eggs to a mixture, break them into a cup or small bowl first, then add them to the mixture.

Rubbing in

1. Use a blunt knife to mix pieces of margarine or butter with the flour. Stir and cut until the pieces are coated with flour.

2. Then, rub the pieces between your fingertips. As you rub, lift the mixture up and let it fall back into the bowl.

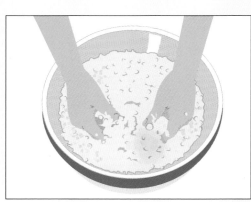

3. Carry on rubbing in the butter or margarine until it is completely mixed in and the mixture looks like fine breadcrumbs.

Beating an egg

Break the egg into a cup or small bowl. Use a fork to stir it quickly until the white and the yolk are mixed together.

Beating a mixture

1. When you beat a mixture, you mix the ingredients really well. First, put the ingredients into a big bowl.

2. Then, stir the ingredients briskly, using a wooden spoon. Carry on until the mixture is smooth and has no lumps in it.

Lining and greasing a cake tin

This stops the mixture from sticking.

1. Put the tin onto a piece of greaseproof paper or baking parchment. Use a pencil to draw around the bottom of the tin.

2. Cut out the shape you drew and put it into the tin. Dip a paper towel into some margarine or butter and rub it over to grease the tin.

Testing a cake

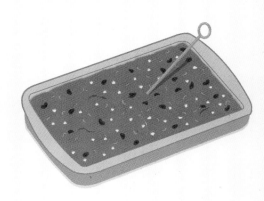

To see if a cake is cooked, push a skewer into it. There should be no mixture sticking to the skewer when you pull it out.

Index

Photographic manipulation by John Russell. Thanks to Kate Fearn, Vici Leyhane and Antonia Miller

First published in 2002 by Usborne Publishing Ltd, 83-85 Saffron Hill, London EC1N 8RT, England. www.usborne.com
Printed in Spain
This edition produced for:
The Book People Ltd, Hall Wood Avenue, Haydock, St Helens WA11 9UL

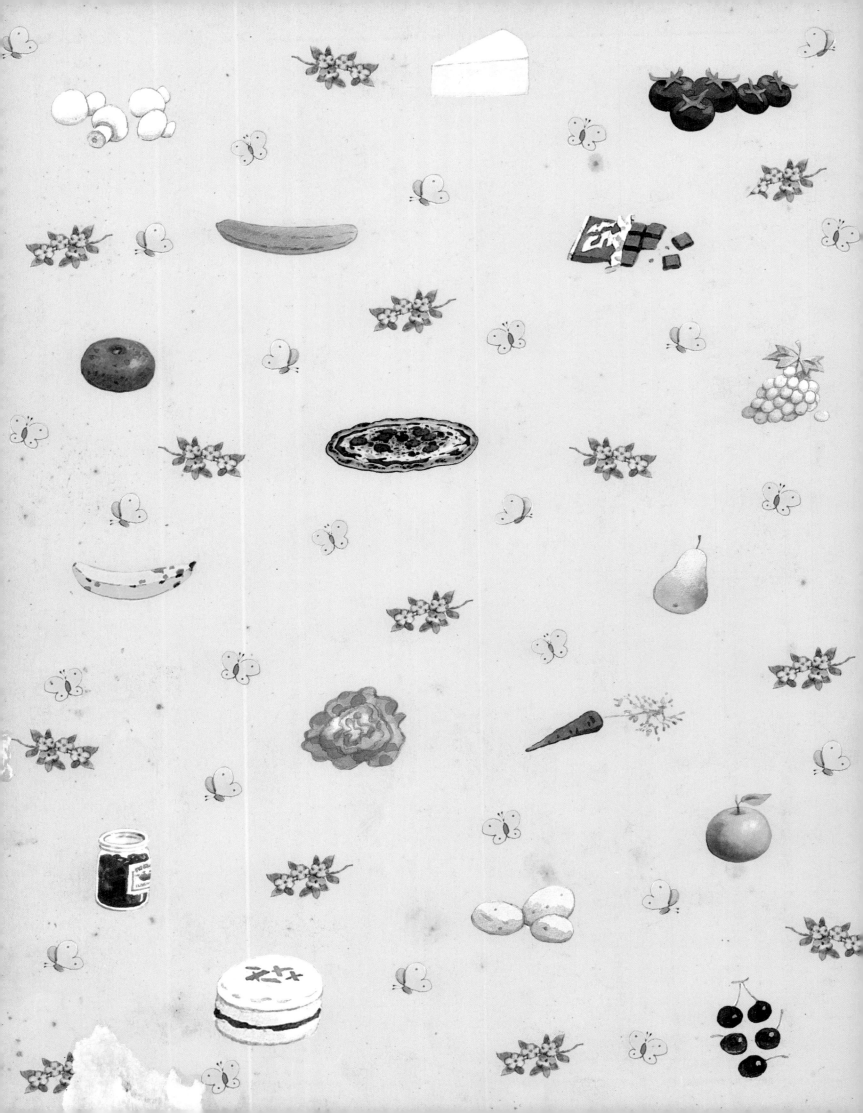